LINCOLN CHRISTIAN COLLEGE AND SEMINARY

J.K. JONES

P9-CPX-821

WHAT THE MONKS CAN TEACH US

AN ANCIENT PRACTICE FOR A POSTMODERN TIME

HEARTSPRING PUBLISHING · JOPLIN, MISSOURI

Copyright © 2004 HeartSpring Publishing
A Division of College Press Publishing Co.
All Rights Reserved
Printed and Bound in the United States of America

All Scripture quotations, unless indicated, are taken from
THE HOLY BIBLE: NEW INTERNATIONAL VERSION®.
Copyright © 1973, 1978, 1984 by International Bible Society.
Used by permission of Zondervan Publishing House.
All rights reserved.

Cover Design by Mark A. Cole

Library of Congress Cataloging-in-Publication Data

Jones, J. K. (John Kenneth), 1953–
    What the monks can teach us : an ancient practice for a postmodern time / by J. K. Jones, Jr.
        p.   cm.
    ISBN 0-89900-491-1 (alk. paper)
    1. Spiritual formation.   2. Monastic and religious life—History.   I. Title.
    BV4501.3.J648 2004
    271'.009'015—dc22

                                                    2004017502

TABLE OF CONTENTS

719

110651

INTRODUCTION
A DESIRE TO CHANGE

Monasticism was and is a living protest against
the secularization of Christianity (J.K. Jones).

The title of the book is strange. Let me admit that from the very beginning. Our postmodern ears are not accustomed to such unusual language. I also acknowledge that the title sounds very Catholic. I am a Christian whose heritage is found in and among Protestants. Some of my spiritual ancestors might be appalled that I would write a book like this or even suggest Catholic monks could be invaluable resources for twenty-first-century Christians. I sympathize with and understand that perspective. Yet, something has happened in my life over the past twenty years that has compelled me to put my thoughts on paper. I have met a group of ancient Christian monks who have blessed and challenged me in ways I cannot totally explain. I want to tell you about how all of this began, but I must first offer some explanation as to what this book is fundamentally about.

This book is about change. Some change is good and some even welcomed. We speak of changing our clothes, our hairstyles, and the oil in the car. We even bask in the changing of the seasons. However, for many of us change

This book is about change.

is a tough, leathery word. It conjures up images of what we don't particularly enjoy doing. Change reminds us of the need to lose weight, reduce cholesterol numbers, or start exercising. There are multitudes of other words in the English language that are much more hospitable and warm

than this one. Words like joy, grace, peace, and hope have found comfortable places in the life of most people within the Church. Most of us are creatures of habit. We like some form of consistency. Even those among us who claim to like variety have a tendency toward wanting a rhythm, a constancy of some kind. But even going to Sunday worship reminds us of the change that is all around us. We once enjoyed finding that same pew, opening the old hymn book, singing those familiar songs, and following a recognizable path of worship. This book will not argue the pros and cons of worship shifts. I simply acknowledge that change exists.

Change that has teeth in it, that carries a price tag, and calls for sacrifice is seldom greeted courteously. Few enjoy a steady stream of strangers knocking at the door. There is satisfaction in the nod of recognition. The problem arises when comfortableness settles cozily into a state of

> Change that has teeth in it, that carries a price tag, and calls for sacrifice is seldom greeted courteously.

complacency. It is not insightful or new to suggest we live in a post-Christian or even pre-Christian culture in North America and in much of the Western World. What is unique is to suggest a means of change within the context of the Church that would aid in liberating evangelicalism from its cultural captivity. The suggested tool of change is a "Protestant form of monasticism." This idea first took seed in my thinking in 1988 when Rodney Clapp wrote an editorial in *Christianity Today*, entitled, "Remonking the Church" (August 12, 1988, pp. 20-21). I've been carrying the concept around in my mind for well over a decade. That article included a discussion about monasticism from three highly distinguished Christian statesmen: John R. W. Stott, Richard Halverson, and Richard Mouw. Clapp recognized that the small, but growing call for remonasticization was and is propelled by the awareness that our situation will not change simply by talking about it. He clearly saw that the American Church finds itself in a culture dominated by consumerism and propelled by a media that encourages and promotes violence, materialism, and sensualism. Even the Church has contracted the disease. It has become increasingly difficult for the Church to maintain its distinctive identity as the Body of the Christ. Clapp soberly reminded us of the amazing ability we have in creating our own celebrities, while claiming we shun the world's stars. At the same time we caution one another not to fall victim to the mania over Wall Street numbers, while developing our own obsession with flow charts, membership rolls, and counting the numbers saved.

It is not enough to be aware that we are in trouble; we must also seek Spirit-directed ways of getting out of trouble. When Israel found itself chin deep in crisis because it rejected the report of Joshua son of Nun and Caleb son of Jephunneh (Numbers 14), the people got up early the next day, acknowledged their sin before Moses and prepared to go to the place the Lord promised. These people were highly motivated and eager to get to work. However, activity has never been a very good substitute for productivity. In spite of Moses' strong caution not to hurry off, "in their presumption they went up," and the enemy that lived there defeated them. What is needed, then, is not more planning. We don't need more programs. Increased busyness is not the answer. Only a rediscovery of the delicate balance between personal piety and community charity, of love of God and love of neighbor, will do. We must position ourselves to listen and follow the eternally articu-

We must position ourselves to listen and follow the eternally articulate voice of God.

I N T R O D U C T I O N

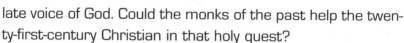

late voice of God. Could the monks of the past help the twenty-first-century Christian in that holy quest?

This book seeks to examine five large questions relating to discovering a biblical form of monasticism. Why the call to remonk the Church? What's behind it? What objections are there to this call? What is Christian monasticism? What are some of the tools available for remonking the Church? How does this kind of change occur? Change is really the business of the Holy Spirit (Barth, *Dogmatics in Outline*, pp. 137-140). All five of the above questions could quite easily be reduced to a program of legalism and "do-it-yourself" Christianity. In contrast, it is extraordinarily freeing to become aware of one's genuine calling to simply be a Jesus follower. Eugene Peterson has devoted much of his writing to reminding the Christian, especially the minister, of his or her vocational calling (see *Five Smooth Stones for Pastoral Work* or *The Contemplative Pastor*). He writes with such surgical precision, both cutting and healing the American pastor with his diagnosis and prognosis. Peterson's plea is for Christian leaders to remain loyal to their call. In Peterson's book, *Working the Angles*, he finds a metaphor from trigonometry that can help in staying tuned to the pastoral call. He describes the visible lines of ministry as preaching, teaching, and administration. The small angles, those that go unnoticed—prayer, Scripture reading, and spiritual direction—are the true angles. These are the genuine angles that can assist in drawing accurate lines for pastoral ministry. We must get the angles right. If working authentic angles is needed, and I believe it is, then all Christians must seek out biblical angles that are true and accurate. God demands it, and the priesthood of all believers needs it! As disciples of Jesus our calling is to first and foremost follow

As disciples of Jesus our calling is to first and foremost follow Him.

Him. Please hear this. The call I'm speaking of is extended to all. At the heart of this book is an invitation to follow Jesus into a storm of grace.

Anytime someone begins to speak of spiritual formation or presenting a "fresh way" of looking at something ancient, an arrogance or lack of humility can slip in covertly. Four temptations faced me as I began writing this book. First, there was the temptation to sound wise. Any Jesus follower who falls under the illusion of believing he or she already knows something fully has entered into that deceptive land called "pride." I have made enough mistakes in my life to know I am not wise apart from the wisdom of Christ. I always want to remain teachable and submissive. The first temptation could have led to a second. There was the temptation to couch this whole discussion in humor. Humor is good and wholesome. It is a barometer for identifying a cheerful heart (Prov 15:3; 17:22). Laughter falls under God's rule and reign (Eccl 3:4). Yet, increasingly, humor has become the numbing spiritual cocaine of shallow messengers. I faced a third temptation. I could have been tempted to dispense answers like a theological pharmacist. The truth is that I am an ordinary man who has more questions than answers. The fourth and final temptation was to identify my own successes in this call to learn from the ancient monks. However, the students I teach and the congregation where I preach could reveal example after example of my own inability to consistently live out the theme of this book.

What I hope to encourage is a longing for God. We must begin with the Father. Two important ingredients should not be forgotten. First, God is self-existing. By His goodness, grace, and love He has desired to make Himself known in a personal way. God's revelation is personal and concrete in the Son, Jesus Christ. Second, because of His willingness to come in flesh, taking on the role of an obedient servant, we now have a theology of the Christian life. God can command obedience because it is not for-

God can command obedience because it is not foreign to Him.

eign to Him (Kettler, *The Vicarious Humanity of Christ and the Reality of Salvation*, pp. 95-96). Our pursuit of God requires a labor of love in placing all of our being before God through a life of devotion and action. I am calling for a voluntary surrender of ourselves to a God who is worthy of exaltation above everything.

In an earlier book that I wrote, *Longing for God*, I briefly tell Nathaniel Hawthorne's classic story, *The Great Stone Face*. It is such an important story to this book I want to retell it in greater detail. Hawthorne describes a people living in a valley, shadowed and surrounded by a huge rock formation. The rocks are shaped together in such a manner that if viewed from a proper distance, a great face can be seen. The face appears divine. It seems to express both warmth and sweetness while embracing all people who look upon it. Hawthorne's main character, Ernest, is a man who has gazed upon the Great Stone Face day after day and year after year. His mother first passed on to Ernest the ancient legend when he was a boy. According to the story there would one day come an incarnation of the great rock. Throughout the narrative rumors surface that a man has appeared who resembles the Great Stone Face. First, Mr. Gathergold, a shrewd and active man whose name identifies his chief ambition in life, is thought to be the fulfillment of the prophecy. Though the people of the valley want to believe that Gathergold is the image of the great face, Ernest knows

he is not. Later a war hero, Old Blood-and-Thunder, is heralded to be the one in whom the likeness is seen. Again, Ernest recognizes what the crowd does not. The general is only a war-worn, weather-beaten hero. Years go by, the people have settled down and now are able to admit the previous two men were not the prophecy's fulfillment. A third character appears in the story, Old Stony Phiz, a man in whom is found a magical oratory skill. His spoken words are like the sweetest music ever heard. As is expected, the people of the valley once again see in this man the Great Stone Face, and once again Ernest is disappointed. Time reveals that Ernest is correct and the people in error. Years pass by. Ernest is quite old. People come to him from all over seeking the understanding of this simple man that cannot be found in books. From college professors to statesmen they visit with this gentle, sincere soul. One last time Ernest hopes he will meet that special one who has been foretold. A poet does appear that Ernest admires greatly, but both the poet and Ernest realize he is not the one. The story closes with Ernest being asked by neighboring villagers to speak to them, and while the golden sun is setting, both the poet and the people recognize what Ernest has not and cannot. Ernest, himself, is the fulfillment of the Great Stone Face! In his humility, constant gaze, and unquenchable seeking he has become that which he sought.

Learning from the monks is not a quick program to be implemented in the life of local congregations or hurriedly incorporated into Bible colleges or university campuses. What this holy undertaking requires is a body of disciples who believe that in humbly gazing upon and seeking the Father in a quiet, godly way they not only can change the Church, and the world, but most importantly, be changed

themselves. "The spiritual life is seldom lived on the plane of the extraordinary. It is for the most part lived amidst the mundane patterns of everyday life, with ordinary people who do ordinary things" (Muto, *A Practical Guide to Spiritual Reading*, p. 109).

The spiritual life is for the most part lived amidst mundane patterns with ordinary people who do ordinary things.

I
N
T
R
O
D
U
C
T
I
O
N

1
UNDERSTANDING THE TIMES

Something is happening here, but you don't know what it is. Do you, Mister Jones? (Bob Dylan, *Ballad of a Thin Man*).

I would be the first to admit I do not always understand what is going on in American culture. I like pondering that line in 1 Chronicles 12:32, ". . . men of Issachar, who understood the times and knew what Israel should do. . . ." The focus of this chapter is to attempt to understand my own times. In the passage quoted above, the Hebrew noun used for "understand" is the word bina. It refers to the faculty or ability to comprehend something fully (Goldberg, *Theological Wordbook of the Old Testament*, pp. 103-104). The Old Testament cautions against trusting in one's own *understanding* (Prov 3:5). Yet, a hearty challenge is given to persist diligently in seeking *knowledge* (Prov 4:5-7). Daniel and his three friends are described as young men who were able to *understand* all that King Nebuchadnezzer asked (Dan 1:20). We don't know much about these "men of Issachar." We do know Issachar was the ninth son of Jacob, mothered by Leah, and had four sons himself who accompanied Jacob to Egypt (Gen 30:18; 35:23; 40:13; Exod 1:3). In 1 Chronicles 12 these men come to David at Hebron knowing clearly what Israel should do in a time of crisis. The context is intriguing. King Saul had banished David from his presence, the Philistines were warring against Israel, religious life was waning, and Samuel was dead! What had started with such great Camelot-like promise now appeared to be ending in catastrophe and despair. However, in those difficult and troubling times there were a few people who studied the culture, grasped its significance, and knew exactly what to do.

The starting point for any comprehension of our times must surely begin with God. We learn about sin by looking at God's holiness. The pleasure and purity of the relationship between God the Father, and Christ the Son, stands in stark contrast to that of the broken relationships in our culture and in the Church. Athanasius, the fourth-century Church Father, was a man of candor who saw the entrenchment of sin and knew what to do. He stressed it was our mind that needed to be redeemed (Torrence, *The Trinitarian Faith*, pp. 164-165). The New Testament agrees. It is our mind that matters the most (Matt 22:37; Rom 1:28; 8:7; 12:2; Phil 3:19; Col 2:18, etc.). Our lawlessness and rebellion can only be changed in and through the Son of God. He is both our substitute for sin and our representative to God. His life is offered for our life. A sweet exchange has occurred (Torrence, p. 179).

> The starting point for any comprehension of our times must surely begin with God.

The mind is being assaulted on every front (2 Cor 4:4). Any discussion about remonking the Church must be seen through the framework of a great spiritual war (Eph 6:10-16). The Scriptures speak of two kingdoms, spiritual in nature, at war against each other (2 Cor 6:14-15; Eph 6:12; Col 1:13). The Bible affirms the reality of this cataclysmic battle and insists the battle cannot be fought in a conventional manner (2 Cor 6:7; 10:4). Of course, many do not believe in a personal devil or demonic forces. Some follow the skepticism of Rudolf Bultmann, a twentieth-century theologian. Bultmann said, "It is impossible to use electric light and the wireless, and to avail ourselves of modern medical

C H A P T E R   O N E

surgical discoveries, and at the same time believe in the New Testament world of demons and spirits" (*Kerygma and Myth*, Vol. 1, pp. 4-5). I believe in "principalities and powers" and the existence of "that immensely powerful, evil and cunning being who is called Satan or the devil" (Stott, *The Cross of Christ*, p. 231). I am not saying he is all-powerful or in any way equal to God. He is not (1 John 4:4). The enemy was decisively defeated at the cross. The war has been won (Col 2:13-15). However, the skirmishes continue and a mortally wounded enemy can be a very dangerous foe (1 Pet 5:8).

The gigantic problems of our day give evidence our culture is eroding. We'll talk about those specific problems in this chapter. Chuck Colson reminds us the crisis is not political, rather it is moral and spiritual. A caution is in order.

> There is a powerful temptation to exaggerate the importance of one's own time. I have no idea whether we face the end of the West or not; history, not to mention the sovereign will of God, is more complex than we imagine. Caution is therefore in order as we attempt to trace the cause of cultural decay. But caution doesn't leave me without convictions. I believe that we do face a crisis in Western culture, and that it represents the greatest threat to civilization since the barbarians invaded Rome (*Against the Night*, p. 23).

Culture is dictating the Church's mission and purpose. I'm not the first to acknowledge this, nor will I be the last. In Corinthian-like fashion the Church is in the process of losing its distinctiveness. We constantly face

Culture is dictating the Church's mission and purpose.

problems of division and disunity in the Body of Christ. We appear afraid, at times, to confront immorality. Within my own

CHAPTER ONE

community I have witnessed Christian suing Christian. The evidence for cultural invasion of the Church could go on and on. These are dark times. This is not to suggest that for the Church to truly be the Church it must always be looking for a fight or churning up the waters of society. On the contrary, when the Church is the Church it recognizes it has been called out of the world (2 Cor 6:14-18) and yet strives to construct bridges of love and witness to that same world (John 13:34-35; Acts 1:8). I admit there are some bright spots in the midst of the darkness. Some are responding to the gospel, and some churches appear healthy and in the business of making disciples. However, it is the overwhelming darkness that makes these glimmers of light seem so bright.

No one is shocked when I acknowledge the Church's flaws. She is, after all, an imperfect Bride. "The New Testament never presents the Church apart from her problems" (Barth, *Dogmatics in Outlines*, p. 142). There was another time in Church history when there was decline and darkness. Between A.D. 500 and A.D. 950 light was nearly snuffed out in the Western world. However, there were radiant glimmers of light shining out of that darkness. A handful of monks were observant, devout, and understood what to do about the darkness. They responded in prayer, study, love, and work, while leading a revolt against the darkness. I'll speak more of that later. For now, what is the darkness that looms over our horizon? What prompts this call to remonk the Church? There are at least six areas of monumental crisis.

Individualism

Eugene Peterson calls our culture a "self-bound society." He recalls the story of the visit of Alexis de Toqueville to

America over one hundred and fifty years ago when he wrote: "Each citizen is habitually engaged in the contemplation of a very puny object, namely himself" (*Earth and Altar*, p. 13).

Everywhere we look, whether in the newspaper, television, or the Internet, individualism is epidemic. Most of us would agree that there is nothing fundamentally wrong with being an individual. It is good to recognize and applaud individual human dignity and uniqueness. Modernity, however, stressed the role of individual freedom to a breaking point. Marriage, the family, and everyday relationships have been weakened in this postmodern age. Gene Veith writes, "The exaggerated individualism that characterizes modernism has split families, with each parent seeking his or her own private identity with no regard for the children, who likewise are left on their own. Ironically, such extreme individual autonomy does not allow for the formation of a strong sense of identity, which is generally formed by nurturing solid families" (*Postmodern Times: A Christian Guide to Contemporary Thought and Culture*, p. 80). The individual becomes de-centered. Robert Bellah says we "have put our own good, as individuals, as groups, as a nation, ahead of the common good" (*Habits of the Heart*, p. 285).

> Everywhere we look, individualism is epidemic.

When individualism works its way into the life of a local congregation, self-preoccupation becomes the gospel of the hour. Now and then I see this selfish preoccupation in a very ugly form. Several years ago a man came to me upset about the lack of prayer before the offering was taken up on Sunday morning. I told him we often did pray before we participated in that portion of our worship service, but not always. His response was shocking.

> Self-preoccupation becomes the gospel of the hour.

C
H
A
P
T
E
R

O
N
E

He promised me that if there wasn't a prayer offered before the next offering time he would keep "his money" and go somewhere else to worship. I don't think it is appropriate to reveal to you what I said in response! I was not mean or combative, just frank. He never once stopped to consider the weight of his words. His self-centered speech was marked with spiritual blackmail. Honesty demands that I confess this sick individualism also lives in me. I'm sometimes surprised and profoundly disappointed in my own intoxication with "me." What individualism means for the Church is that we often have fewer resources for penetrating the world with the Good News of Jesus.

What individualism means for the Church is that we often have fewer resources for penetrating the world with the Good News of Jesus.

Benedict (480–543) was one of the most famous monks in Church history. He was the founder of the monastery at Monte Cassino and authored the now famous *Rule*. Benedict truly was the father of Western monasticism. His early attempts to build a community of priests who would live together in stability, humility, and spirituality were not successful. However, his own spiritual growth and desire for cooperation and flexibility eventually bore fruit at Monte Cassino and around Europe. Through his adaptable *Rule* monasteries became great "centers of learning, agriculture, hospitality, and medicine in a way presumably unforeseen by Benedict himself" (Farmer, *Oxford Dictionary of Saints*, p. 47). Self-preoccupation gave way to selfless service. Perhaps the monks of the past could help us all challenge the monstrous crisis of individualism.

Perhaps the monks of the past could help us all challenge the monstrous crisis of individualism.

Materialism

Materialism follows closely on the seductive heels of individualism. Jesus' followers must regularly ask themselves, "Am I managing the possessions God has entrusted to my care, or are my possessions man-aging me?" In the Church there is a disturbing greed that is evidenced by the attention we give to financial concerns, budget

"Am I managing the possessions God has entrusted to me, or are my possessions managing me?"

plans, and administration of funds, rather than on Scripture, prayer, and evangelism.

I am at a place in my life where I reflect a great deal on what God has entrusted to my care. I have many things, but I don't want those things to have me. For example, I love motorcycles. I always have. There is something unexplainably wonderful about being on the open road, away from the phone, riding along without a care in the world. Every time I look at a new Harley, especially a Heritage Softtail, I wonder if it is not time to give in to that desire and buy one. I look at the price tag and just about gag. Then I take a glance at my nine-year-old bike. It still looks good. It still has a lot of good road time left in it. Soon I talk myself out of owning one more thing. I like how A.W. Tozer once put it. "There is the sweet theology of the heart which can be learned only in the school of renunciation" (*The Pursuit of God*, p. 27).

There was once a monk by the name of Bede (673–735) whose life might help us defeat the dragon of materialism. He never traveled far. He never owned much of anything. From the age of seven to the end of his life he was educated by monks and lived in the monastery of Jarrow, England. He read, studied, and wrote his twenty-five volumes of Scripture commentary. He lived simply, humbly, and quietly so as to help as many as he could through his vast writings (*Oxford Dictionary of Saints,* pp. 45-46). Calvin Miller is absolutely correct. "Having is not the first sin of materialists. The sin that precedes it is, the sin of regarding what we have as our own" (*Into the Depths of God,* p. 38). Bede never focused on his writings as being his own or "getting ahead," but on imitating Christ. Modern materialism could learn much from the simple life of monasticism.

Spiritualism

The third challenge of our time is spiritualism. Spiritualism, as defined in this book, is the idea of people arriving at what they mean by "faith" on their own terms. Spiritualism should not be confused with "spirituality." By spirituality I mean a devotion to Jesus Christ. Spiritualism, on the other hand, "signifies the belief that truth is located in the inward Spirit or inner light" (Donald Bloesch, *The Crisis of Piety,* p. 53). The final authority of spiritualism resides in the person, but the ultimate authority in spirituality rests in the revelation of God, both the Living and Written Word.

There is a monstrous paganism located in the worship of the human will.

There is a monstrous paganism located in the worship of the human will. In the book of the Judges there is a repeated line that clearly identifies the crisis I'm attempting to describe. Listen to this revealing refrain: "Everyone did as he saw fit" (17:6; 21:25). Whatever Israel felt like doing, she did. Of course, the anarchy and chaos that followed was not surprising. I appreciate the subtle and creative way Os Guinness describes counterfeit Christianity. In his imaginative work, *The Gravedigger File.* Guinness, like C. S. Lewis before him in *The Screwtape Letters,* reveals the Enemy's objective.

Our aim in them all is the same: to ensure that the church is shaped rather than shaping, reverting to the pattern of its culture rather than renewing its culture after the pattern of the Adversary (here Guinness refers to Christ, p. 138).

Boniface (675–754) was one of the great English missionaries educated in monasteries. He wrote the first Latin grammar used in England. He was a bold and persuasive preacher and evangelist among the pagan tribes of Germany. In order to challenge the false gods of his day he once chopped down a sacred oak tree to show those same pagan gods could not stand against the gospel or protect those who trusted them. Many came to faith in Christ through his courageous ministry (*Oxford Dictionary of Saints*, pp. 63-64). I believe monks like Boniface, who served Jesus during the early years of the Middle Ages, display for us the difference between spiritualism and spirituality.

Violence

Anything is permissible when God is no longer acknowledged as the center of reality. Violence is certainly one of those possibilities. Who would disagree that this specific crisis permeates our society from playground to battleground? Hollywood cinema, local newspapers, and our Sony televisions remind us daily of the violence that floods our world. In our culture a secular humanistic philosophy has taken on a religious fervor. There is a deep-rooted paganism found in the worship of the human will. We are fascinated and hypnotized by power. Violence literally covers the multifaceted media of our day. Perhaps the most disturbing thing is the manner in

> Anything is permissible when God is no longer acknowledged as the center of reality.

C H A P T E R   O N E

which television has become the principal mode of our culture's knowing about itself. Few have grasped the implications of television like Neal Postman. In *Amusing Ourselves to Death* Postman chillingly tells us, "How television stages the world becomes the model for how the world is properly to be staged" (p. 92). Television conditions us to tolerate most anything. To those of us who are troubled by all of this violence, we hear repeated promises from politicians and lawmakers that they will soon correct the problem. These are false promises.

Television conditions us to tolerate most anything.

I, too, battle the addiction of watching violence on movie screen and television screen. I lead and participate in a small accountability group at the college where I teach. Sometimes I ask this question of the group: Have you been anywhere, seen anything, done anything, or said anything that is not God-honoring? Before they respond I must break the silence with a humble confession of my own, "Yes," I say. "I watched violence on television last night and was seduced by it." I replay a scene in my mind where a student inflicts violence on another student. In shame I admit that I want to avenge that violence with even more violence. I thank God for the example of Peter Damian (1007–1072). He began life with great difficulty. Damian lost both his mother and father when he was just a child. He then suffered abuse at the hands of one brother before he was adopted by another. Damian eventually became a monk in 1035. Peter Damian grew to become a preacher, pastor, poet, spiritual director, and peacemaker. He once brought a fighting, divided congregation together and helped them settle their differences in the spirit of Christ. Damian also assisted Henry IV and his wife avoid an immi-

C
H
A
P
T
E
R

O
N
E

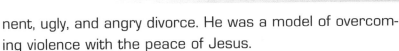

nent, ugly, and angry divorce. He was a model of overcoming violence with the peace of Jesus.

Sensualism

Sensualism weighs heavily on contemporary culture. When experience and feelings are elevated as gods, one's sexuality simply becomes a means of expressing sexual desire. We face a culture that worships the god of the loins. We have moved deeper and deeper toward self-centeredness. This is not to say that people in general are mean; on the contrary, they are generally nice. But this is a strange sort of nice. It is a nice that is not very deeply rooted. It is a camouflaged cover for getting what one desires. Allan Bloom observes that the change in sexual relations came upon us in two large tidal waves. First, there was the wave of the sexual revolution, and second, there came the wave of feminism. The former marched under the banner of freedom, the latter under the flag of equality. "The uneasy bedfellowship of the sexual revolution and feminism produced an odd tension in which all the moral restraints governing nature disappeared, but so did nature" (Bloom, *The Closing of the American Mind*, p. 105). AIDS still threatens our society. Teenage pregnancy remains a problem. Experimentation with sexual relationships outside of marriage continues to pose imminent danger for the family and the American culture. The Internet daily devours Christian and non-Christian alike. This should not surprise us since 60% of all web sites are devoted to some form of pornography and sexual seduction. Elizabeth Elliot offers a keen insight into this demonic crisis.

> We face a culture that worships the god of the loins.

In forfeiting the sanctity of sex by casual, nondiscriminatory "making out" and "sleeping around," we forfeit something we cannot well do without. There is a dullness, monotony, sheer boredom in all of life when virginity and purity are no longer protected and prized. By trying to grab fulfillment everywhere, we find it nowhere (*Passion and Purity*, p. 21).

Augustine (354–430) provides assistance for this looming challenge. He was the child of a Christian mother and an unbelieving father. He later studied rhetoric at Carthage, North Africa. Augustine originally prepared to be a lawyer, but became a teacher instead. Though raised a Christian, he denied faith in Jesus. For fifteen years he lived with a mistress and through that relationship fostered an illegitimate son. Eventually Augustine ended that relationship and was baptized into Christ on Easter Sunday, April 25, 387, by Ambrose, after a long and difficult inner journey. He was ordained a priest in 391 and ultimately became the Bishop of Hippo where he led a monastic life. His writings help us honestly face the temptations and snares of sexual seduction that live in all of us. Augustine's *Confessions* especially prove invaluable.

I wish to bring back to mind my past foulness and the carnal corruptions of my soul. This is not because I love them, but that I may love you, my God. Out of love for your love I do this. . . . I came to Carthage where a caldron of shameful loves seethed and sounded about me on every side. I was not yet in love, but I was in love with love, and by a more hidden want I hated myself for wanting little. I sought for something to love, for I was in love with love; I hated security, and a path free

C H A P T E R   O N E

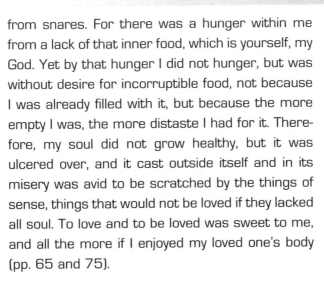

from snares. For there was a hunger within me from a lack of that inner food, which is yourself, my God. Yet by that hunger I did not hunger, but was without desire for incorruptible food, not because I was already filled with it, but because the more empty I was, the more distaste I had for it. There-fore, my soul did not grow healthy, but it was ulcered over, and it cast outside itself and in its misery was avid to be scratched by the things of sense, things that would not be loved if they lacked all soul. To love and to be loved was sweet to me, and all the more if I enjoyed my loved one's body (pp. 65 and 75).

There must always be a place for a gritty, transparent spiri-tuality. Admittedly, Augustine's life precedes the Dark Ages, but his example of confession and transformation remains timeless. He models for us a way out of the sensual mess.

Christian Secularism and Pragmatism

One more observation will suffice for the necessary call to remonk the Church. This final challenge may be one of the most diabolical and devastating for the community of believ-ers. This giant is a two-headed monster comprised of Christian secularism and pragmatism. The kind of secular-ism I'm talking about is the kind that advances only as ortho-doxy retreats. The god of pragma-tism is the clearest evidence for the onslaught of secularism. The criteri-on, in many churches, for evaluating "success" is "Does it work?" The apparent conclusion is, if something works, it must be right. How do we fight this par-ticularly American heresy? What do we do about it?

The criterion, in many churches, for evaluating "success" is "Does it work?"

CHAPTER ONE

The worst thing possible is to attempt to do something myself, to tinker around with various programs or plans. The place to begin is self-surrender. I must come back to Scripture and become Word-driven. I must dive deeply into the life of God as found in Christ. I must believe in the fact that God can show me what He is doing and what I can do in turn to partner with Him. Calvin Miller sobers me and encourages me all at the same time. I believe he understands this two-headed giant of secularism and pragmatism. Listen.

> How often the church is like Gilligan's Island. Christians aren't really living on the edge. The church doesn't encourage them to break out of their insular spirituality. In fact, the best way to live comfortably as believers is to accept island living. . . . Recently a very popular study called "Experiencing God" swept through the church. It is a very beautiful, demanding, and profitable study. But I began to notice that many of those who enrolled in the Experiencing God study course, weren't reading *Experiencing God* and then talking as if they had actually experienced God. It seemed an odd substitution to let the study of it serve as the experience. But it is fashionable these days to talk about how deep we are while we live on a "Gilligan's Island" of church life. . . . I see the church not as an armory where we plan our conquests of fire, but as bunkers — island bunkers — where the furniture is nice and faith is a discussion. . . . Gilligan's Island might more properly be called Cape Fear. We huddle in the cleft of the rock to avoid the storms, not to stand on the craggy heights and let them exhilarate us (*Into the Depths of God*, pp. 226-227).

**C
H
A
P
T
E
R

O
N
E**

Willibrord (658–739) was a priestly monk who was passionate in his preaching and gracious in his ministry. He was a man whose life was marked by prayer and sacred reading. His work and witness were joy-filled and gracious. Willibrord later became the Bishop of Utrecht and baptized many into Christ. Church historians credit him with converting the countries of Luxembourg and Holland to Christianity in spite of the moral decay of Europe. I love how David Farmer puts it, "Willibrord's pioneering work, which inaugurated a hundred years of English Christian influence on the Continent, was of great importance and he thoroughly deserves his title of patron of Holland" (*Oxford Dictionary of Saints*, p. 511). I mention Willibrord because he shines as a soldier of Christ against the dark Cyclops of secularism and pragmatism that had penetrated the church in his day. He was an evangelist who preached the gospel wherever and whenever he found people who did not know Jesus.

Dietrich Bonhoeffer understood the challenge of his day. "It is becoming clearer every day that the most urgent problem besetting our Church is this: How can we live the Christian life in the modern world" (*The Cost of Discipleship*, p.60)? Bonhoeffer's question is our question. It is a question that is both joy-filled and demanding. It is joy-filled because it calls us to Jesus. It is demanding because it calls us to not succumb to the world. Monasticism was and is a living protest against the secularization of Christianity.

C
H
A
P
T
E
R

O
N
E

2
MONASTICISM'S PROBLEM: MONKS AND THEIR MESSES

Hearts aflame with mercy, like the sun in midnight sky,
while the doubter shrugs his shoulders and the cynic wonders why
(Bob Bennett, *Still Rolls the Stone*).

Let's face it honestly and squarely, the monks did not always "shine like stars in the universe" (Phil 2:15). Sometimes they were as boneheaded and sinful as those who did not claim to be Christians. Sometimes they were as belligerent and rebellious as I am. Again, it doesn't surprise most of us for me to acknowledge that we find ourselves in a mess, both in the culture as well as in the Church. There is not a single, pleasant way of saying this without it hurting a bit. Before we delve into the messes that the monks sometimes created, let's consider what gave rise to the monastic call.

Kenneth Latourette's fine book, *Christianity through the Ages*, helps me understand what contributing factors brought about the rise of monasticism. First there was a nominal allegiance to Jesus which began in A.D. 312 at the conversion of Constantine. Assisting this secularization was the deterioration of Rome due to the inner sickness of its society. Finally, there was the appeal of the ascetic tradition in the early Church that fostered a climate of indifference toward the ethical call of the gospel (Latourette, pp. 35, 73, and 100). Due primarily to the last factor, it must be admitted there were bizarre forms of asceticism that surfaced. I acknowledge that there were abuses in the monastic movement.

Historians like to refer to Simeon (Symeon) Stylites

(398–459) as an example of a strange and extreme form of monasticism. The word *stylite* comes from the Greek word *stulos*, which means "pillar." Simeon was known as one of the "pillar saints." These pillar saints were monks who chose to live a solitary life on top of a pillar. The pillars varied in height and were sometimes large enough that a small hut could be built on top. Necessities, such as food and water, were provided by followers or admirers. While living on top of their pillar, these "stationary monks" would devote themselves to prayer, spiritual direction, conflict resolution, and dealing with theological controversies (*Oxford Dictionary of the Christian Church*, p. 1317). Simeon lived on his pillar for approximately thirty-six years. He, on one occasion, while back down on solid ground, dug a trench in a garden and daily buried himself in it up to his head through an entire summer (Walter Workman, *The Evolution of the Monastic Ideal*, p. 42). Monks like Simeon were not seeking a revolution or reconstruction of society and the Church, rather they were seeking the salvation of their own souls (Workman, pp. 11-12).

Some monks chained themselves to rocks in caves or in public spaces where people could see them each day. Other ascetics lived in old cisterns, while subsisting on only five figs a day (Workman, p. 44). Still others lived without clothing only covering their bodies with their own long, uncut hair. Some hung weights around their necks, or placed themselves in cages, or ate but once a week, or only ate kneeling, or only drank water drawn from the dew that was collected from rocks. Some monks stood while sleeping. Some lived in swamps, abandoned caves, or even tombs. Some never bathed. In all of this misplaced asceticism there was a passion to renounce self and seek to please God (Workman, pp. 44-45).

We know Christians of earlier times, like Origen (105–254), mutilated themselves, believing that Matthew 19:12 ("For some are eunuchs . . .") must be interpreted literally. Monks like Origen led strict ascetic lives of prayer, fasting, vigils, and voluntary poverty. One of the most famous abuses in monastic history was the tragedy that befell Peter Abelard (1079–1142). Peter was in love with a woman by the name of Heloise. He was a brilliant thinker and popular teacher on the staff of the Paris Cathedral School. Two conflicts changed his life. First, he placed high prominence on man's ability to reason, pitting himself against Anselm (1033–1109), a Benedictine monk and Archbishop of Canterbury. Anselm believed faith was a precondition for understanding. Abelard, a powerful debater, angrily disagreed with Anselm. Specifically, the two leading monks fought over the meaning and significance of Christ's death on the cross. Anselm placed the emphasis on the work of Christ, while Abelard placed the emphasis on our response to the work of Christ. Abelard not only had the ability to present his ideas with passion, but he also had the ability to cause people to respond to him in anger. The second conflict was even more explosive. Canon Fulbert of Notre Dame found out his niece, Heloise, was having an affair with Abelard. Though we are uncertain as to the exact age of Heloise, she was probably somewhere between the age of fifteen and seventeen.

Ruth Tucker, in *Christian History*, presents one of the finest and most illuminating portraits of the love affair between Heloise and Abelard. Tucker says the affair unfolded in three stages. First, there was the seduction of Heloise by Abelard, who served as her tutor. Heloise found herself pregnant. It was not long before her uncle, Fulbert, also discovered the awful truth of her affair and subsequent pregnancy. In bitter anger, he plotted revenge against Peter by hiring friends to carry out judgment against Abelard. One dark night avengers slipped into Abelard's bedroom and castrated him! In the second stage of the story Abelard came to the sober realization of his deplorable life, repented, and left the university to live the monastic life. Heloise blamed herself. Peter, in turn, then helped Heloise through her own brokenness and encouraged her to enter a monastic life as well. In the third and final stage Abelard went through a series of problems with the Church and was charged with heresy. He died before he reached Rome to make his appeal to the Pope.

When I speak of remonking the Church I am not advocating the strange perversions and asceticism that sometimes existed in the Middle Ages. I admit those messes occurred. I appreciate the honesty of Thomas Cahill in his marvelous work, *How the Irish Saved Civilization.*

> Tales of solitary ecstatics and madmen remained as abundant as ever, whether of Sweeney, the king who thought he was a bird and lived his life in treetops, or of Kevin of Glendalough, a sixth-century hermit who lived in a hole in the rock wall of a cliff, emerging in winter to stand for hours stark naked in the icy waters of the lough or in summer to hurl himself—again naked—into a bush of poisonous nettles (p. 156).

There is little doubt that abuse, darkness of soul, and doctrinal confusion abounded. However, those same ingredi-

C H A P T E R   T W O

There is little doubt that darkness of soul and doctrinal confusion abounded but those same ingredients exist in our times.

ents exist in our postmodern times. So what are some of the contemporary objections to calling twenty-first-century Christians into a new monasticism?

Objection #1: Two-Tiered Christianity

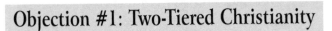

First, there are those who will suggest that remonking the Church would create another two-level Christian community. Once again, we would cause some to feel like second-class citizens in the Kingdom. The ancient struggle between clergy and laity would continue. Some would suggest the watching world would be confused as to what it means to be a Christian. My response to this first objection is to simply acknowledge the problem already exists. What's new? If remonking the Church meant only those who took vows of celibacy, poverty, and charity could participate, then the objection would be legitimate. But I am talking about a different kind of monastic recovery. I'll explain what I mean in greater detail in a later chapter.

I am talking about a different kind of monastic recovery.

Martin Luther (1483–1546), the Augustinian monk, spent torturous years struggling over his own salvation. In his exploration and study of Romans he discovered and experienced the radical grace of God in Christ. The papal sale of indulgences for the building of St. Peter's basilica in Rome ignited the newborn reformer to challenge the theory of penitential favors. In 1517 he wrote his *Ninety-five Theses* declaring, among other things, that the Pope had no jurisdiction over purgatory. The German Reformation was birthed. As the movement grew, Luther wrote numerous essays, one of which addressed the concern of this two-level Christianity. In *The Babylonian Captivity of the Church* Martin Luther discusses the seven sacraments of the Roman Church, devoting most of the treatise to the problem of the Lord's Supper and Baptism. As he argues for abolishing vows and elevating faith and baptism, he writes:

> Therefore I advise no one to enter any religious order or the priesthood, indeed, I advise everyone against it—unless he is forearmed with this knowledge and understands that the works of monks and priests, however holy and arduous they may be, do not differ one whit in the sight of God from the works of the rustic laborer in the field or the woman going about her household tasks, but that all works are measured before and by faith alone. . . . Indeed the menial housework of a manservant or maidservant is often more acceptable to God than all the fastings and other works of a monk or priest (*Three Treatises*, pp. 202-203).

Though not directly intending to assault a two-tiered Christianity, Luther blows apart any notion that one's fervor or zealousness is more acceptable than another's in God's eyes. The criticism leveled against remonking the Church, built upon the notion of creating a two-class structure, falls mute. There has consistently, through biblical history, been a stark contrast between genuine followers and those "along for the ride" (Num 13:26–14:4; John 6:60-71).

Objection #2: Pride

A second objection to remonking the Church might be the inevitable birth of pride and aloofness among those who would follow this ancient way. Perhaps an Essenelike, isola-

tionist mind-set would creep in. I agree that the heart is deceitful above all things (Jer 17:9). However, numerous biblical passages caution against this treacherous sin of pride. Instead, Scripture honors humility (Phil 2:3-4; Col 3:12-14; Jas 4:10; 1 Pet 5:5-6; and 1 John 2:15-16). Benedict, in his *Rule*, highlighted twelve steps of humility and discipline.

> The first step of humility . . . is that a man keeps the fear of God always before his eyes (Ps 36:2) and never forgets it. . . . The second step of humility is that a man loves not his own will nor takes pleasure in the satisfaction of his desires; rather he shall imitate by his actions that saying of the Lord: I have come not to do my own will, but the will of him who sent me (Jn 6:38). . . . The third step of humility is that a man submits to his superior in all obedience for the love of God, imitating the Lord of whom the Apostle says: He became obedient even to death (Phil 2:8). . . . The fourth step of humility is that in this obedience under difficult, unfavorable, or even unjust conditions, his heart quietly embraces suffering and endures it without weakening or seeking escape. . . . The fifth step of humility is that a man does not conceal from his abbot any sinful thoughts entering his heart, or any wrongs committed in secret, but rather confesses them humbly (Ps 37:5). . . . The sixth step of humility is that a monk is content with the lowest and most menial treatment, and regards himself as a poor and worthless workman in whatever task he is given (Ps 73:22-23). . . . The seventh step is that a man not only admits with his tongue but is also convinced in his heart that he is inferior to all and of less value (Ps 22:7).

The eighth step. . . . is that a monk does only what is endorsed by the common rule of the monastery and the example set by his superiors. . . . The ninth step of humility is that a monk controls his tongue and remains silent, not speaking, unless asked a question (Ps 140:12). . . . The tenth step of humility is that he is not given to ready laughter, for it is written: Only a fool raises his voice in laughter (Sir 21:23). The eleventh step of humility is that a monk speaks gently and without laughter, seriously and with becoming modesty, briefly and reasonably, but without raising his voice. . . . The twelfth step of humility is that a monk always manifests humility in his bearing no less than in his heart, so that it is evident at the work of God, in the oratory, the monastery or the garden, or on a journey or in the field, or anywhere else. . . . Now, therefore, after ascending all these steps of humility, the monk will quickly arrive at that perfect love of God which casts out fear (pp. 32-38).

Obviously, to the twenty-first-century reader some of these steps are troublesome, but at the heart of Benedict's counsel is the recognition of the subtle manner in which pride can seep into the armor of Christ's soldier. In a magnificent sermon, entitled *Human Greatness under the Judgment of Love*, Dietrich Bonhoeffer confronts anyone who would be duped into thinking too highly of themselves. "The world order is turned upside down when it takes these words seriously, 'and have not love, I am nothing.' These words cut deeply into our own ranks, our church, who did not keep the marriage between personal piety and community charity" (*A Testament of Freedom*, p. 255). Augustine echoes that same conviction as He speaks of Jesus' working in our inner lives. "He heals their

swellings, and nourishes their love, so that they may not go on further in self-confidence, but rather become weak" (*Confessions*, p. 176). Simply admitting that all of us are vulnerable to the seduction of pride is a first step toward escaping the trap of arrogance.

> Simply admitting that all of us are vulnerable to the seduction of pride is a first step toward escaping the trap of arrogance.

Objection #3: Isolation

Some critics of monastic practice would say that monks isolated themselves from society. It is true that some monasteries did withdraw from the world. It is important to remember the Eastern wing of the Catholic Church was far less oriented toward engaging the world in preaching, teaching, and shepherding. I don't want to be guilty of overstatement, but the Western monk was less inclined toward complete isolation. The Eastern monastic withdrew and remained almost entirely untouched and unchanged. In the West monasteries became the very center of culture, civilization, and education. This became one of the great reasons why so many women entered the convent of the Middle Ages. Nowhere else could women have access to libraries and learning as they did in the monastic orders (See Jo Ann McNamara, "Inside the Convent," in *Church History*, 1991, vol. 10, no. 2, pp. 19-21). In the East an almost barren asceticism led to little contribution in life and service (Workman, *The Evolution of Monasticism*, pp. 150-162).

I admit there were those in monastic history who did not keep the marriage between personal piety and community charity. However, that same divorce lives on today. There are those contemporary followers of Jesus who hide away from culture and never live as salt and light. I have, at times, been

guilty of this very divorce. The balance between devotion and service is best exemplified in Jesus. He often withdrew for prayer, solitude, and refreshment in order to be

There are those contemporary followers of Jesus who hide away from culture and never live as salt and light.

even more attached to the great needs of the world (Mark 1:35-39; Luke 5:16; 9:10-11). One of the fine writers of our time, Glandion Carney, reminds us of the essential interplay between time alone with God and time in service to people.

> The tension between the contemplative life of spiritual exercise and the active life in the day-to-day world will never go away. But I have found ways to keep them in balance. . . . True spirituality is a structure which successfully blends internal values with outward commitments. Spirituality is not an escape from the world. Rather it's a holiness which is practical and relevant to the world we live in. . . . [Spirituality] is a rhythm of life that moves inwardly and outwardly (*Heaven within These Walls*, pp. 43 and 45).

Donald Bloesch says, "The purpose of withdrawal should be a more radical penetration into the citadels of the world" ("A Call to Spirituality" in *The Orthodox Evangelicals*, p. 156). The activity of God within us, His work of sanctification, will consistently and constantly develop a deep love and passion to act on Christ's behalf in the world as we cooperate with His purposes. If we are to re-monk the church in the twenty-first century, there will be a

If we are to remonk the church, there will be a well-worn path between withdrawal from the world and engagement of the world.

well-worn path between withdrawal from the world and engagement of the world.

|Objection #4: Too Catholic|

There will always be those who see any talk about learning from the monks as too Catholic. I recognize there are some Protestant evangelicals who are extremely uncomfortable with any notion that might hint of anything that sounds pre-Reformation. They rightly state: "I thought we wanted to restore New Testament Christianity to the contemporary Church. Forget the Middle Ages, let's simply focus on the first century." I don't disagree with the important business of restoring the Church to New Testament Christianity. My own heritage is deeply committed to that very principle (The Stone-Campbell Movement). The problem, though, is multifaceted. What part of the New Testament are we talking about? Not everything recorded in the letters to the early churches is worthy of imitation. There were divisions, immorality, false teachings, lawsuits, and various other sordid problems.

> Tragically, we so often focus on two centuries of Church history, the first one and the one we are living in.

Tragically, we so often focus on two centuries of Church history, the first one and the one we are living in. I must constantly fight the urge to see God's activity reduced to only a two-hundred-year period with a sprinkle of Reformation, sixteenth-century style, thrown in. I believe that every period of Church history has something of value to teach me. Even the early Middle Ages had some shining lights that illuminated the culture for Christ.

So what exactly is Christian monasticism? Perhaps some of the monks of the past can best explain that and in the process become mentors for us.

3

CHRISTIAN MONASTICISM: A WORLD OF MENTORS

The central question becomes, how will we live a life capable of hearing the "still small voice" of God, while experiencing the speed and sensory overload of modern life? How does one hear God's voice in the twenty-first century? (Corinne Ware, *Saint Benedict on the Freeway*, pp. 15-16).

I have searched for the perfect mentor since my high-school days. I know I sound like a naïve Ponce de Leon. Regardless, I think Maxwell and Dornan are right, "Mentors impact eternity because there is no telling where their influence will stop" (*Becoming a Person of Influence*, p. 123). Years after high school, when I was preaching and serving a local congregation, I would have given up my salary to find a mentor that could help me through the sticky and thorny problems of ministry. Somewhere in the late seventies and early eighties I providentially stumbled onto the writings of Richard Foster. I don't think I can put into words what exactly happened, but this I know, I became hungry for more. One book on the spiritual disciplines led to other books and soon I was noticing footnotes about devotional classics and writers. I began to work my way through the thick, lush rain forest of spiritual giants. Many of them I have read very slowly. My relationship with those monks and nuns has, at times, been filled with ecstasy, like being alone with my best friend, my wife. I have hungered to be with them, intimately, quietly grateful to simply listen. Some, truthfully, I have read swiftly. I just didn't find a connection. The problem, I am sure, is on my side of the equation. I have felt myself avoiding a few of the monks and nuns like I might avoid a draining

→

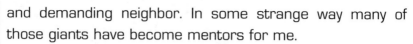

and demanding neighbor. In some strange way many of those giants have become mentors for me.

Mentoring is intentional. It does not happen by chance. "Mentors major in guiding, encouraging, and teaching, not in controlling" (Weidmann and White, *Spiritual Mentoring of Teens*, p. 70). I love the biblical narratives that describe this kind of relationship. The Bible, perhaps you've noticed, is filled to the brim with examples of these life-changing experiences. Consider Jethro and Moses (Exodus 18); Moses and Joshua (Deuteronomy 31); Eli and Samuel (1 Samuel 2); Jonathan and David (1 Samuel 18–20); Elijah and Elisha (1 Kings 19 and 2 Kings 2); Jesus and the 12 (the Gospels); Barnabas and Saul (Acts); Paul and Timothy (Acts 16 and 1 and 2 Timothy); Paul and Titus (2 Corinthians 7 and Titus). There is a deep and abiding hunger for that kind of investment and transformation in the hearts of a lot of people. A mentor or spiritual director is someone with whom we can be accountable. This relationship includes confidentiality, gratitude, and spiritual stimulation. The objective in all of this is Christian maturity. Of course, it does not happen quickly.

> Mentoring is intentional; it does not happen by chance.

Every semester, at Lincoln Christian College, someone comes up to me and asks, "Would you mentor me?" It is a breathtaking moment. Often that student doesn't even know what they are really asking. Often I am not sure what I can really offer. Even more often I have to decline their request. I already have several people with whom I am committed to mentoring. Most of my colleagues are in the same over-crowded boat. I teach at an institution that desires to prepare Christian leaders. Our stated mission is "to prepare servant leaders to know Christ and to make Him known to the world." How is that possible without some form of men-

C
H
A
P
T
E
R

T
H
R
E
E

toring? The problem, obviously, is that there are very few who are willing and prepared to take on the time required and commitment needed to disciple another person. Mentors have to have the space to ask the hard questions and listen for the answers that follow. For example: What is your relationship with God like? How is God testing you these days? What evidence is there that you are experiencing His presence and power? What has been painful for you recently? Where and when have you experienced joy in your journey? What has been going on in your prayer life? Are you closer to Jesus now than at your conversion? Have you been anywhere, seen anything, said anything, or done anything that has not been God-honoring? Where has God been speaking to you from Scripture? When you look into the mirror at your own face what do you see that you like and what do you see that you deplore? Have you cried over anything in the past year? Have you laughed hard and long over anything in the past week or two? The list of questions could go on and on.

There are very few who are willing and prepared to expend the time and commitment to disciple another person.

Mentors are not necessarily dispensers of answers. They are, though, an extra set of ears and eyes to the mysterious storm of God's grace. They help us listen for God's presence and activity. It seldom enters the mind of most people to consider finding a mentor who has been dead for some time. I know that sounds insane. It is not what usually comes to mind when we think of a mentoring relationship. Eugene Peterson was the first person who got me thinking about the legitimate place of a dead mentor. Let me explain. Peterson made it a holy habit to set aside time each week to read and meditate on the writings of great Christians of the

C
H
A
P
T
E
R

T
H
R
E
E

past. He treated those encounters as weekly appointments. Month after month, year after year, he quietly listened to their words, their lives, and their questions. If you have ever read any of the many writings of Peterson you know that he expresses himself with great depth and insight. He has been profoundly shaped by the great spiritual classics, by Luther, Calvin, Barth, Dostoyevsky, and many others. I cherish the story he tells in *Take and Read*.

> I have a friend who became a Christian as a young adult, and then was ripped off and exploited by unscrupulous, predatory religious leaders. Disillusioned, he wandered off into the world of alcohol and drugs and spent the next twenty years trying to get his spirituality from chemicals. One day in the mountains of Mexico, on a hunt for drugs, he met some drug dealers who had recently become Christians. They talked to him about Jesus, prayed for him, and he reentered the Christian way. Back home in Canada, he knew he needed support in his new life, but because of his earlier experience with religious leaders, he was wary. One day he went into a bookstore and asked the manager, "Do you have any books by dead Christians? I don't trust anybody living." He was given a book by A. W. Tozer, and for the next year read nothing but Tozer—"a dead Christian." From there he cautiously worked himself back into the company of living Christians, in which he is now a most exuberant participant (pp. xi-xii).

**C
H
A
P
T
E
R

T
H
R
E
E**

Tozer was the prototype for someone who understood what

it meant to remonk the church. This Protestant Christian searched and studied the great devotional classics. He meditated on and applied what he learned from the monks and nuns. He was a pastor and preacher for decades in Chicago and later in Toronto. His many writings are anointed with insight and wisdom. If I wanted to be mentored by someone who modeled personal piety and community charity, I would turn to the vast writings of Tozer.

If I wanted to be mentored by someone who knew how to continually pray and live out an awareness of God's presence, I would seek out Brother Lawrence. He could actually become a guide for me in nurturing my own spiritual receptivity. I would read and reread *The Practice of the Presence of God*. It is absolutely amazing to me

It seldom enters the mind of most people to consider finding a mentor who has been dead for some time.

that a fumbling and bumbling seventeenth-century monk could have so much to say about giving simple attention to God. This uneducated Jesus follower washed dishes and prepared food in such a way that God was ever present in all that he did. Thank heaven that his fellow monks compiled Lawrence's words and practices.

If I wanted to be mentored by someone who could help me to become more childlike, I would get as close to St. Francis of Assisi as I could. When I read and meditate on *The Little Flowers of St. Francis,* I often laugh out loud at the way in which Francis engages all of life. He preached to the birds, rejected materialism, engaged the marginalized, and lived with genuine humility. I need extended time with this thirteenth-century monk. Even if I don't accept as factual some of the miracles associated with Francis, I am still blessed by his playfulness and innocence.

C
H
A
P
T
E
R

T
H
R
E
E

If I wanted to be mentored by someone who could assist me in persevering through times of great difficulty and suffering, I would try to read as much of Madame Jeanne Guyon as possible. She was a French Christian who endured the abuses and tyranny of seventeenth-century Catholicism. Guyon's nearly two decades of prison experience produced not only a refined inner character, but a beauty that went beyond the physical body. The publishing house of Bridge-Logos, in their Pure Gold series, has updated into modern English many of the great devotional classics, including the writings of Jeanne Guyon.

If I were looking for a mentor who could teach me about the goodness of God, I would run to Julian of Norwich. If I wanted to find a spiritual guide to help me not only learn how to confess my sins, but to confess my love for God and celebrate His grace, I would get as close to Augustine or Patrick of Ireland as I could. If I wanted to grasp how wide, how deep, how long, and how high is the love of God, I would establish regular appointments with Bernard of Clairvaux. If I ached to know Jesus and in turn imitate Him through a radical commitment, I would devour Thomas à Kempis and *The Imitation of Christ*. If I wanted spiritual guidance in how to daily live a life of devotion I would sit down regularly with Michael Molinos or Francis De Sales. If I wanted to live a life of full obedience to Jesus, if I wanted to call a fractured world and divided Church to the peace that only Jesus can bring, I would listen closely to the life and words of Catherine of Siena (1347–1380). If there was an ache in my soul for living a life of simplicity, I would make regular visits to hear Clare of Assisi (1194–1253).

Perhaps a word from a nonmonk might help support what I am trying to convey. A.W. Tozer openly acknowledged

C
H
A
P
T
E
R

T
H
R
E
E

the mentoring he received from the great ones of the past. Not all the people he mentions are monks or nuns, but they are monklike in their love and passion for God.

> Some of the great names are Meister Eckhart, Bernard of Clairvaux, Jan van Ruysbroeck, Michael Molinos, John of the Cross, Thomas Traherne, Richard Rolle, William Law, Walter Hilton, Francis de Sales, Jakob Boehme and Gerhart Tersteegen. To those might be added the more familiar names of Fenelon, Guyon, and Thomas à Kempis. To a large extent these were universal Christians who experienced the grace of God so deeply and so broadly that they encompassed the spiritual possibilities of all men and were able to set forth their religious experiences in language acceptable to Christians of various ages and varying doctrinal viewpoints. . . . Theoretically the people of God should run to these books as a thirsting stag runs to bury his muzzle in the cooling stream; actually only a relatively few welcome them (*The Size of the Soul*, pp. 46-48).

Now and then, when I become self-preoccupied, I bemoan the fact that I haven't found the perfect mentor. Sometimes I let this foolish thought slip out into conversation with a friend or two. Not long ago I confessed to a cherished colleague my ache over being mentorless. Please don't misunderstand. I have plenty of people around me, good people, mature people, who have sharpened me and helped me in my walk with Jesus. I don't have that spiritual director who asks just the right question, at just the right time. I'm assuming most of us don't have that kind of person in our lives. As

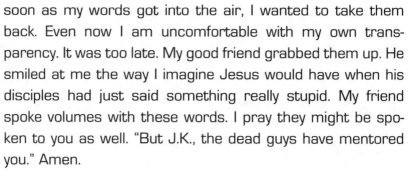

soon as my words got into the air, I wanted to take them back. Even now I am uncomfortable with my own transparency. It was too late. My good friend grabbed them up. He smiled at me the way I imagine Jesus would have when his disciples had just said something really stupid. My friend spoke volumes with these words. I pray they might be spoken to you as well. "But J.K., the dead guys have mentored you." Amen.

C
H
A
P
T
E
R

T
H
R
E
E

4
MONKS AND
THEIR TOOLS

That living Spirit pressing so insistently on our spirits, filling with its
spaceless presence every room of the soul's house, yet comes to us in
and through natural circumstance; and makes of this circumstance,
however homely, the instrument of its purifying power. . . . God comes
to the soul in His working clothes and brings His tools with Him. . . .
It is not a week-end cottage. It must be planned and organized for life,
the whole of life, and not for fine weather alone (Evelyn Underhill,
Concerning the Inner Life and The House of the Soul, pp. 99-100).

I wish I had greater skill with tools. I'm fairly credible with
the gardening kind, but when it comes to the mechanical
or carpentry variety, I am rather inept. Not long ago the sink in
our kitchen began to leak. I went down to the local hardware
store and purchased all the necessary items. The store owner
was kind enough to talk me through the process and even told
me to call him if I ran into trouble. He must have been a
prophet or the son of one, because I never did stop that leak.
My wife had to telephone the plumber down the street to come
and rescue me. It was embarrassing. He not only had the right
tools for the job, he knew how to use them.

I have, for some time, appreciated the words of Evelyn
Underhill quoted above. Her words conjure up for me a picture
of God in His bib overalls coming to work on my soul with His
toolbox in hand. She creates an image of earnestness and
grace for me. God loves me so much He
continually remodels and renovates my
heart into His home. What really intrigues
me is the invitation He extends to me to
work alongside of Him in this great under-

God loves me so much
He continually remodels
and renovates my heart
into His home.

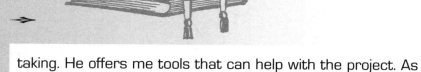

taking. He offers me tools that can help with the project. As time goes by and I gain some experience, I become fairly skilled and proficient with those tools.

So what are some of those instruments God willingly places in my toolbox?

> He offers me tools that can help with the project.

Today we refer to these tools as spiritual disciplines. They include meditation, scriptural intake, fasting, prayer, worship, and many others. These are time-tested means of working alongside of God in order to become more like His Son, Jesus. "The disciplines allow us to place ourselves before God so that He can transform us. . . . By themselves these disciplines can only get us to the place where something can be done" (Richard Foster, *Celebration of Discipline*, p. 6). Richard Foster calls this undertaking, "the way of disciplined grace." "It is 'grace' because it is free; it is 'disciplined' because there is something for us to do" (p. 6). When we recognize what God has done for us in Christ, there is a response that gives proof to whether or not we have truly grasped God's gift to us. The proof rests in how we cooperate with God's desire to transform us into Jesus' likeness.

One of the monks from the past understood all of this. I have mentioned him earlier. His name was Benedict. Though we don't know much about Benedict, we do owe a debt of gratitude to Gregory the Great, who was Pope from 590 to 604. Gregory tells us something about Benedict in his *Second Book of Dialogues*. He informs us that Benedict was born in Nursia, Italy, a village located in a mountainous area northeast of Rome. We also know, through Gregory, that Benedict studied rhetoric and law in Rome, but was more interested in serving God through a monastic lifestyle. For three years Benedict lived as a hermit in a cave and was

CHAPTER FOUR

fed daily. A loaf of bread was lowered by a cord into his cliff-side monastery. Some of the chapters in Gregory's account speak of miracles attributed to Benedict. The one matter, though, that has allowed this ancient monk to remain known even today is His *Rule*. He saw the communal monastery as

> . . . a school for the Lord's service. In drawing up its regulations, we hope to set down nothing harsh, nothing burdensome. The good of all concerned, however, may prompt us to a little strictness in order to amend faults and to safeguard love. Do not be daunted immediately by fear and run away from the road that leads to salvation. It is bound to be narrow at the outset. But as we progress in this way of life and in faith, we shall run on the path of God's commandments, our hearts overflowing with the inexpressible delight of love. Never swerving from His instructions, then, but faithfully observing His teaching in the monastery until death, we shall through patience share in the sufferings of Christ that we may deserve also to share in His kingdom. Amen. (*Prologue* 34-47, pp. 18-19).

The *Rule* (*RB*) is simply a written guide showing how a Jesus follower can live in intimacy with God while journeying through an imperfect world. I love the gracious way he concludes the last chapter. ". . . All these are nothing less than tools for the cultivation of virtues; but as for us, they make us blush for shame at being so slothful, so unobservant, so negligent. Are you hastening towards your heavenly home? Then with Christ's help, keep this little rule that we have written for beginners" (*RB* 72.6-72.8, pp. 95-96).

Tool: Love of God and Neighbor

Benedict offers at least eight tools that can be helpful to the church in the twenty-first century. His first tool is love for God and neighbor. He reminds us that our way of acting should be different from that of the world's way. With the gentleness of a caring shepherd he says, "If you notice something good in yourself, give credit to

> Our way of acting should be different from that of the world's way, but we do not have to make this complicated or difficult.

God, not to yourself" (*RB* 4.42, pp. 27-28). He describes with simplicity and clarity how this love for God and neighbor is lived out through our words and our silence, through our work and our rest. We do not have to make this complicated or difficult as a daily spiritual exercise. We can simply use this tool by meeting with the Lord each day in prayer, Scripture reading, and worshiping. We could practice it by simply seeing Jesus in others and carrying out random acts of kindness and love.

Tool: Renouncing Self

His second tool is renouncing self. He cautions against pampering "self." Antony, earlier, had applied his understanding of renouncing one's self by fasting continually.

> His clothing was hair on the inside while the outside was skin, and this he kept to his dying day. He never bathed his body in water to remove filth, nor did he as much as wash his feet or even allow himself to put them in water without necessity. No one ever saw him undressed, or did anyone ever look upon his bare body till he died and was buried (Athanasius, *The Life of St. Antony*, p. 47).

Benedict described this kind of humility as not loving one's own will nor taking pleasure in the satisfaction of one's desires (John 6:38). In the monastery no one was to follow his own heart's wish. A genuine monk cared, submitted, endured, and was content with the lowest and most menial treatment or work. I find that kind of selflessness difficult. I need daily reminders to keep this tool close at hand. Foster describes this kind of submission as, "the abili-

> I find the kind of selflessness that cares, submits, endures, and is content with the lowest and most menial treatment or work difficult.

ty to lay down the terrible burden of always needing to get our own way" (*Celebration*, p. 97). It is why, I suppose, I'm drawn to Barnabas's willingness to sell a piece of property he owned (Acts 4:36-37), Dorcas's willingness to show active compassion for the poor (Acts 9:36), and Paul's willingness to put the churches' interests ahead of his own (2 Cor 11:23-28). Simply allowing someone else to go ahead of me at the stop sign or in the grocery store checkout counter can keep this tool cleaned and sharpened.

Tool: Observing

The third tool Benedict speaks of is clearly connected to the second. He describes it as "noticing," "keeping careful watch," "listening readily" (*RB* 4:41, 48, 55, pp. 27-28). Earlier in the *Rule* Benedict challenges himself and his fellow monks to "open our eyes to the light that comes from God, and our ears to the voice from heaven that every day calls out this charge: 'If you hear His voice today, do not harden your hearts' (Ps 95:8). What, dear brothers, is more delightful than this voice of the Lord calling to us" (*Prologue*, 9-10 and 19, pp. 15-16)? For the sake of brevity I will refer to this tool as "observing." Within the monastic movement there is a strong sense of God's presence. Benedict puts it succinctly, "We believe that the divine presence is everywhere" (*RB* 19.1, p. 47). There is an acute awareness among the monks that as they pray they

Within the monastic movement there is a strong sense of God's presence.

know that God is doing something through that single prayer in the whole Body of Christ. Basil Pennington says, "These hours of watching come to be among the most prized hours of the monk's life" (*Light from the Cloister*, p. 37).

"Praying without ceasing" clearly is the primary means of observing God at work (Matt 26:40; Mark 1:35; Luke 6:12; Ps 130:5-6). The loving means for using this tool is through praying with my eyes wide open. I practice this each morning as I take my daily walk, praying about what I see and asking God to help me to recognize His presence in what I will encounter that day. I was thinking about this one morning when I watched my neighbor's small boy head off to his first day of school. The bus pulled up at 7:00 a.m. sharp. Both parents escorted their son from the front steps of their house to the school bus. I watched them kiss and hug him good-bye. He never looked back to wave from the bus window. I saw the parents wipe tears from their eyes as they headed back to the house. It made me think about how much God misses us when we busily move through our day. Who couldn't regularly observe and ponder such moments?

Tool: Prayer

Prayer is the fourth tool. The intentional kind of prayer Benedict describes differs from the kind mentioned above. It is the kind that is devoted to praying for enemies and praying for mankind. It is the kind of prayer that is wedded to huge chunks of reading. This *lectio divina*, reading with God

in mind, became a way for hearing God, meditating on His words, responding in prayer and finally resting in contemplation. This tool of prayer was a way of both talking and listening to God. Kierkegaard grasped what Benedict meant.

> This the true man (and woman) of God knows well. . . . In proportion as he became more and more earnest in prayer, he had less and less to say, and in the end he became silent. He became silent—indeed, what is possible still more expressly the opposite of speaking, he became a hearer. He had supposed that to pray is to speak, he learnt that to pray is not merely to be silent but to hear. And so it is, to pray is not to hear oneself speak, but it is to be silent, and to remain silent, to wait, until the man who prays hears God (*Christian Discourses*, p. 323).

To pray is not to hear oneself speak, but it is to be silent, and to remain silent, to wait, until the man who prays hears God

The daily regimen of the monks was shaped by the hours of prayer and reliance upon the Psalms as the guide for prayer. Phyllis Tickle's, *The Divine Hours*, can put concrete application on the use of this tool. She has taken Benedict's "fixed-hour praying" and crafted a very usable resource for blending prayer and praise three times a day. Anybody can do this.

Tool: Obedience

The fifth tool, interspersed through the *Rule*, is that of obedience. Benedict said, "In the monastery no one is to follow his own heart's desire" (*RB* 3.8, p. 26). Imagine what might happen if every Christian sought to apply that principle in his own place of influence. Benedict refers to obedience as the first step of humility. For the monks this tool was primarily used in two ways: obedience shown to superiors and obedience shown through keeping the fear of God (*RB* 5.1–7.10, pp. 29-32). Obedience was held in highest regard by the monastery. All forms of obedience were seen

> Obedience was held in highest regard by the monastery. All forms of obedience were seen as offerings to God.

as offerings to God. The monks found tremendous freedom in this. They did not have to be preoccupied with worry and fret, but could simply get on with whatever they were asked to do by the Abbot. The *Rule* freed them to live out the example of Jesus (Phil 2:6-11).

Now and then, at the college where I teach or the church where I preach, someone goes out and does something really stupid. I've been guilty of that very thing myself. Some people take their freedom in Christ and use it as a license to do whatever they want. Of course, that kind of decision inevitably causes the name of Jesus to be dishonored and innocent people to be hurt. It also leads to painful self-hurt. I have sat on the disciplinary committee of two Bible colleges. I know how tormenting it is to watch someone willfully reject this essential tool to a healthy Christian life. I have wept with students who long with all their heart to take back a moment of disobedience. I realize the church must always guard against demonic legalism, but I also realize that same church must forever be on guard against seductive licentiousness.

There are some minimal rules we should establish for ourselves in order to live out a God-honoring life. The prob-

> I realize the church must always guard against demonic legalism, but I also realize that same church must forever be on guard against seductive licentiousness.

lem, of course, is that Bible colleges usually have an established set of rules that everyone is asked to follow. Some churches even have such rules. I seek to adhere to one rule and one rule only. I can state it as a question: will this honor Jesus? I'll live with the accusations that I'm being too simplistic and too childlike. What would you have to do differently right now in order to allow the monks to teach you a thing or two about obedience?

> I seek to adhere to one rule and one rule only. I can state it as a question: will this honor Jesus?

Tool: Silence and Solitude

Benedict's sixth tool combines silence and solitude. I love the way he puts it. Good works are to be left unsaid out of esteem for silence.

> . . . Indeed, so important is silence that permission to speak should seldom be granted even to mature disciples, no matter how good or holy or constructive their talk . . . the disciple is to be silent and listen. . . . Let there be complete silence. No whispering, no speaking—only the reader's voice should be heard there (meal time). The brothers should by turn serve one another's needs as they eat and drink, so that no one need ask for anything (*RB* 6.2-3, 6 and 38:5-6, pp. 31 and 60).

In matters of solitude Benedict reminds all those who seek the monastic life, "The workshop where we are to toil faithfully at all these tasks is the enclosure of the monastery" (*RB* 4:78, p. 29). The monks applied the desert motif of John the Baptist and Jesus to come away and be alone (Matt 3:1-4 and 4:1-11). They understood solitude makes the way for

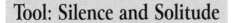

**C
H
A
P
T
E
R

F
O
U
R**

the possibility of silence. Henri Nouwen said, "Silence is the way to make solitude a reality" ("Silence: The Portable Cell" in *Sojourners*, July, 1980, p. 22). Obviously, silence and solitude coexist. I'll talk more about this later. For now, they are a double-edged tool for surgically removing spiritual cancer. Silence and solitude cut and heal. In this way they assist us in knowing God more deeply and fully. Whether we seek exterior or interior silence and solitude, the results can be miraculous. I think this is what Thomas Merton came to understand.

> Silence and solitude cut and heal; they are a double-edged tool for surgically removing spiritual cancer.

> It is in deep solitude that I find the gentleness with which I can truly love my brothers. The more solitary I am, the more affection I have for them. It is pure affection, and filled with reverence for the solitude of others. Solitude and silence teach me to love my brothers for what they are, not for what they say (*The Sign of Jonas*, p. 261).

Because life is so noisy, those who wish to truly learn from the monks must pick up this tool and follow their example. We don't have to retreat to monasteries, but we do have to retreat. All we have to do is get to our calendars first before someone else does.

> We don't have to retreat to monasteries, but we do have to retreat.

Tool: Moderation in Eating

In a world that is consumer-mad the seventh tool will prove quite helpful: moderation in eating. David Knowles observes that fasting and abstinence are not infallible tests for holiness, but history and spiritual experience suggest

that a monastery could be roughly gauged by its diet. In the Middle Ages meat was allowed only in the infirmary or at the Abbot's table when guests were being entertained (Knowles, *Christian Monasticism*, p.118). Benedict offers his usual practical advice by suggesting two kinds of cooked food be served, with fruit or fresh vegetables when available, along with bread and moderate drink. He saves his view for one pointed statement: "Nothing is so inconsistent with the life of

"Nothing is so inconsistent with the life of any Christian as overindulgence."

any Christian as overindulgence" (*RB* 39:8, p. 62). Benedict recommended one meal a day, in the evening. The beauty of the monastic meal is found in the daily reading of Scripture as the meal was eaten with thanksgiving. As I noted earlier, only the voice of the one reading Scripture was heard at the table.

Over the years, I have deeply appreciated the solidly biblical and exceptionally helpful chapter Richard Foster wrote on fasting in *Celebration of Discipline*. I encourage its reading in light of this tool. One of the practical ways we can implement the teaching of the monks is by moderating our eating through a periodic fast. Along with Foster, Dallas

"Fasting unto our Lord is therefore feasting—feasting on Him and on doing His will."

Willard's perspective has been invaluable to me. "Fasting confirms our utter dependence upon God by finding in Him a source of sustenance beyond food. . . . Fasting unto our Lord is therefore feasting—feasting on Him and on doing His will" (*The Spirit of the Disciplines*, p. 166).

All of this moderation and fasting talk doesn't mean that there is no longer any room for celebration and feasting. Jesus feasted and fasted (Luke 5:27-35; Matt 4:1-11). Our Lord's chief caution about fasting pertained to using it legalistically for displaying one's piety (Matt 6:16ff). A possible application for this tool might be as elementary as leaving the dinner table slightly hungry, rather than completely full. I appreciate Basil Pennington's reminder.

> When we fast and know the pangs of hunger we are in compassionate communion with our desperately hungry sisters and brothers in the ghettos and Appalachians of our own country as well as in the blighted corners of the globe. Out of the emptiness of each of us as individuals comes a fullness for all of us together (*Light from the Cloister*, pp. 103-104).

Jesus followers do practice moderation in the absence of their Bridegroom. The great feast is yet to come! Sometimes in order to remind myself of these truths I will fast a twenty-four-hour period, from sunset to sunset. It is relatively painless and doesn't disturb the rhythm of my family and home. Because of health reasons some may not have the physical ability to employ this tool into the rhythm of their inner life. Most people, though, could enrich their walk with Jesus through moderation and fasting.

Tool: Work

For the monks life became a spiritual vocation. They cleared land, put it into cultivation, built bridges, roads, and hospitals. Manuscripts were copied. Art and music were created. Study, especially, was viewed as work. Reading, the call to explore the depths of Scripture and good books, was highly encouraged. Benedict elevates this no less than eleven times in the *Rule* (*RB* 48:1-25, pp. 69-70). He said,

C
H
A
P
T
E
R

F
O
U
R

"When they live by the labor of their hands, as our Father and the Apostles did, then they are really monks. Yet, all things are to be done with moderation" (*RB* 48:8-9, p. 69). From serving in the kitchen to caring for the sick, work was viewed as a means of worship.

I can't help but wonder what difference this tool might make in a Christian's life as he or she goes off to work. Paul

From serving in the kitchen to caring for the sick, work was viewed as a means of worship.

saw its significance, "Whatever you do, work at it with all your heart, as working for the Lord, not for men. . . . It is the Lord Christ you are serving" (Col 3:23-24b). Brother Lawrence included this

tool as a part of his spiritual chest. He made it his life ambition and aim to cultivate the presence of God in the kitchen where he cooked and scrubbed pots and pans. In the noise and clutter of the kitchen his prayer stands as an encouragement to anyone who is willing to learn.

> Oh my God, since Thou art with me, and I must now, in obedience to Thy commands, apply my mind to these outward things, I beseech Thee to grant me grace to continue in Thy Presence, and to this end, do Thou prosper me with Thy assistance, receive all my works, and possess all my affections (*The Practice of the Presence of God*, pp. 24-25).

Antony of Egypt, according to Athanasius, sang Psalms, studied, fasted, prayed, rejoiced in the life to come, labored in order to give alms, grew a garden so as not to burden others, and made his own bread. Centuries later a monklike Christian by the name of Dietrich Bonhoeffer studied, wrote, taught, preached, prayed, stood with the oppressed, practiced the disciplines, "always had time for this brethren," and

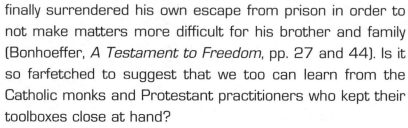

finally surrendered his own escape from prison in order to not make matters more difficult for his brother and family (Bonhoeffer, *A Testament to Freedom*, pp. 27 and 44). Is it so farfetched to suggest that we too can learn from the Catholic monks and Protestant practitioners who kept their toolboxes close at hand?

C
H
A
P
T
E
R

F
O
U
R

5

BEING THE WAY
WITHOUT BEING IN THE WAY

Patrick's gift to the Irish was his Christianity—the first
de-Romanized Christianity in human history, a Christianity without
the sociopolitical baggage of the Greco-Roman world, a Christianity that
completely inculturated itself into the Irish scene. . . . A Christian culture,
where slavery and human sacrifice became unthinkable, and warfare,
though impossible for humans to eradicate, diminished markedly
(Thomas Cahill, *How the Irish Saved Civilization*, p. 148).

We need a "Christianity which antagonizes culture without denying its place" (Bonhoeffer, *A Testament to Freedom*, p. 26). There is something about that statement that resonates with my spirit and my desire to be more and more like Jesus. The monks have this amazing ability to teach us how to be the Way of Jesus, without getting in the way of Jesus. That possibility, alone, excites me! The kind of life I've been trying to describe is a pilgrimage, not a program. One of the aspects of monastic life that I have come to admire is the consistent desire to bring about reform and renewal. Even though there are doctrines that these monks held that I do not, I remain stirred by their desire to honor Jesus. Western monasticism, particularly, went through a number of "revivals" each attempting to help the Church to recover the essential duet of devotion and action. Seven of the major monastic orders were, at times, sources for these periodic "awakenings." There are at least forty-five different monastic orders today (See Helen Walker, *Knights of Christ*, pp. 472-475).

> The kind of life I've been trying to describe is a pilgrimage, not a program.

The Benedictines, who were sometimes called the "Black Monks," preferred to work in local churches and reform them from the inside out. They kept much of Western society's organization during the Barbarian invasions. They have been credited with saving priceless pieces of art and restoring many of those treasures. The Augustinian monks, on the other hand, tended to be hermits or friars. They concentrated their work in small towns and villages. The Carthusian monks were strictly contemplative and took vows of silence. Each monk had his own cell or hermitage where he prayed, worked, and meditated. They sought to live without any formal *Rule*. Historically they seem less affected than the other orders when monastic decline occurred. Cistercian monks are sometimes referred to as the "White Monks." They built their monasteries in remote areas and lived together in community fashion. This group of monks took great delight in designing monastic architecture that was unadorned. That same perspective influenced the simple and plain design of their clothing. The Cistercians followed strict guidelines in diet, silence, and labor. The Franciscan monks took complete vows of poverty. They supplied their own needs through manual labor or through begging. They were absolutely forbidden to own property or accept money for their own personal use. An eventual split occurred in the order over the ownership of property. The Dominicans were a group of monks who sometimes were called the "Black Friars." This was due to the black mantle they wore over their white habit. They elevated intellectual pursuits in their ministries and especially focused their work among the universities of the day. The academic world was their mission field. Finally, there were the Jesuits. These monks were fiery apologists for the faith and militant mis-

sionaries of the gospel. Each one of these monastic orders attempted reform and restoration.

A group of monks came out of the Benedictine order which I greatly admire. They were called "anchorites." Benedict describes them as Christians . . .

> who have gone through the test of living in a monastery for a long time, and have passed beyond the first fervor of monastic life. Thanks to the help and guidance of many, they are now trained to fight against the devil. They have built up their strength and go from the battle line in the ranks of their brothers to the single combat of the desert. Self-reliant now, without the support of another, they are ready with God's help to grapple single-handed with the vices of body and mind (*RB* 1:3-5. p. 20).

These anchorites gave themselves wholeheartedly to a life of sacrifice and prayer. They often built small huts or sheds next to the wall of a church building. The anchorites were comprised of both men and women. Ann Warren wrote an excellent article entitled, "Five Religious Options for Medieval Women." In that article she tells us the "anchoress" was a faithful solitary who tied together withdrawal and religious service. Even how these men and women built their small homes preached to the watching community. Often one window was placed in their small hut, looking out to the world, in order to symbolize deep concern for the culture. A second window was sometimes added, looking into the church building, in order to symbolize equal concern for the church. A few of those tiny homes had three windows. . . . "One for light, one into the church for receiving communion, and one to the outside" (Warren). Bravo!

The word "anchorite" comes from a Greek word, *ana-choreo*. It expresses the idea of intentionally withdrawing. In the New Testament *anachoreo* is used to describe the *escape* of Joseph and Mary to Egypt in order to flee from the tyranny and threat of Herod (Matt 2:13). It is also inserted into the biblical story to tell us how Jesus *withdrew* from the people who wanted to make Him king by force (John 6:15). *Anachoreo* is used in a similar way when Jesus was compelled to *withdraw* because the Pharisees were plotting to kill Him (Matt 12:15). Sometimes Jesus simply *withdrew* for seasons of prayer (Mark 3:7). These ancient anchorites can teach us how to stay anchored to the church, while comprehending and ministering to the needs of the culture.

As I study the life of the monks, I love concentrating on the example of Jesus. He appears to me as the true anchorite. In the hurry and worry of our day as we find ourselves becoming infected by the culture around us, Jesus offers at least three antibiotics. First, he offers the antibiotic of solitude.

The Antibiotic of Solitude

Others, like me, have experienced the way in which solitude dismantles our scaffolding. It strips away all the artificial props of our life, those things I tend to place my trust in rather than Jesus. My Lord, over and over again, retreated for times of prayer and reflection (Mark 1:35; 6:30-32; 6:46-47; 7:24, etc.). Hurry is a menacing and terrorizing threat to the inner life. We do not have to

> Hurry is a menacing and terrorizing threat to the inner life; it is only through solitude that we can continue to care for people.

belong to a monastery to wage the good fight against it. We do, however, have to have regular times of withdrawal. It is only through solitude that we can continue to care for people. I notice in my own life that my tenderness and sensitivity toward others only increases as I regularly seek extended times of quiet and centering.

The Antibiotic of Silence

The second antibiotic Jesus offers is silence. Of course, solitude and silence are inseparable twins. We discussed this earlier. Silence, though, has a distinctive work apart from solitude. Silence discloses my superficiality. When I am in a constant hurry, I am totally vulnerable to spiritual and ministry shortcuts. I look for the quickest way to fix a problem or prepare my next teaching or sermon. Silence sorts out all the cultural propaganda I am so easily tempted to follow. I have often wondered what Jesus talked about as He and the disciples walked from place to place. I have come to a conclusion of sorts that I cannot support biblically. There is just not enough evidence. I believe that a lot of those travel times were spent in silence, allowing greater clarity and focus to take place for the times when Jesus did speak. I don't know if my conclusion is accurate or not. I simply know when Jesus was standing before Pontius Pilate and had the opportunity to defend Himself, He chose to remain silent (Matt 27:13-14; Mark 15:3-5). He appears to me as having practiced that same discipline long before that fateful day.

Silence discloses my superficiality.

The Antibiotic of Simplicity

Jesus offers simplicity as a third antibiotic to the disease of hurry. Simplicity deadens my self-absorption. It helps me surrender all my playthings. One of our area newspapers will run a CitiBank advertisement periodically. The advertise-

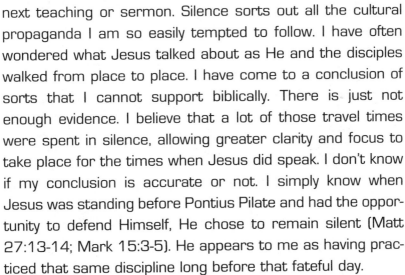

ment reads: "He who dies with the most toys is still dead." Jesus shows me it is possible to fight against the alluring sirens of money, lust, the desire to be first, to be noticed, and to be in charge (Matt 4:1-11; Luke 4:1-13). He shows me a way out of that deadly spiderweb through a spirit of gratitude for what He has given me, through the faithful practice of whole-life stewardship, and through the simple act of charity toward others. What Jesus does for me is to show me that I don't have to reject the way of Jesus in order to do the work of Jesus! He is the perfect anchorite!

Who among us doesn't get in a hurry sometimes? Who among us hasn't tried to fix the problem ourselves? My oldest daughter and I were on an extended mission trip several years ago. We traveled from the United States to Australia to Papua, New Guinea, back to Australia and finally to New Zealand. Toward the end of our weeks away from home we were leaving the airport in Auckland, New Zealand. We found ourselves hurrying to catch a bus that would drive us from the domestic terminal to the international one. We located our bus and were attempting to board when we noticed an elderly couple loaded down with a heavy suitcase. They, too, were attempting to get from the domestic side of the airport to the international side. I handed Lindsey our bags and got her a seat and then went to help this couple. When I stepped out of the bus, I realized they didn't have just one heavy bag to load, they had six heavy bags! I have no idea what they had packed, but I have wondered since if everything they were lugging around with them was necessary. At times, seeing them struggling to carry their luggage reminds me of all the unnecessary weight I carry around with me.

No one ever really arrives at perfection when it comes to solitude, silence, and simplicity. We simply keep growing,

keep striving, and by the transforming power of the Spirit, we make progress. We can become a Christian who has gone through the test of living for a long time and is now trained to fight against the devil. We become a part of the Way, without being in the way.

No one ever really arrives at perfection when it comes to solitude, silence, and simplicity. We simply keep growing, keep striving, and by the transforming power of the Spirit, we make progress.

C
H
A
P
T
E
R

F
I
V
E

CONCLUSION
A JOURNEY
WORTH TAKING

The lives of great Christians show that they differed not only from each other but from themselves at different periods of their lives. Spiritual exercises that helped them at one stage of their development later became useless and had to be changed for others. To stay free from religious ennui (boredom) we should be careful not to get into a rut, not even a good rut (A.W. Tozer, *That Incredible Christian*, p.109).

Sometimes I wonder if I am making any progress at all in the Christian life. I battle the same temptations that I battled when I first surrendered my life to Jesus. I, occasionally, stumble into the same snares and booby traps the enemy constructed against me when I was just beginning to understand spiritual warfare. I would despair if not for the evidence of God's grace at work in my life. Every Jesus follower experiences staleness and fatigue periodically. It is what we do about that dryness that defines our true character. These days I find myself in a continuing dialogue with some of the great Christians of the past. Tozer has reminded me to pursue this conversation with all my heart and soul.

> Every Jesus follower experiences staleness and fatigue periodically. It is what we do about that dryness that defines our true character.

Why do some persons "find" God in a way that others do not? Why does God manifest His presence to some and let multitudes of others struggle along in the half-light of imperfect Christian experience? . . . All He has ever done for any of His children He will do for all of His children. Pick at random a score of great saints

whose lives and testimonies are widely known. Let them be Bible characters or well-known Christians of post-biblical times. You will be struck instantly with the fact that the saints were not alike. Sometimes the unlikenesses were so great as to be positively glaring. How different, for example, was Moses from Isaiah; how different was Elijah from David; how unlike each other were John and Paul, St. Francis and Luther, Finney and Thomas à Kempis. . . . Their differences must have been incidental and in the eyes of God of no significance. In some vital quality they must have been alike. What was it? I venture to suggest that the one vital quality which they had in common was spiritual receptivity. Something in them was open to heaven. . . . They had spiritual awareness and they went on to cultivate it until it became the biggest thing in their lives (*The Pursuit of God*, pp. 66-67).

That pursuit is the journey worth taking. I don't think I could continue on unless I had experienced travelers at my side. The monks have proven to be invaluable traveling partners for me. They tend to point out the things for which I should be watching and listening. Toward the end of Tozer's, *The Pursuit of God*, he asks this essential question.

Now, someone may ask, "Is not this of which you speak for special persons such as monks or ministers who have, by nature of their calling, more time to devote to quiet meditation? I am a busy worker and have little time to spend alone." I am happy to say that the life I describe is for every one of God's children

C O N C L U S I O N

regardless of calling. It is, in fact, happily practiced every day by many hard working persons
and is beyond the reach of none (p. 95).

I have come to deeply appreciate skilled writers like Tozer. Somewhere in my reading pilgrimage I heard about a group of writers who are a part of something called The Chrysostom Society. The society is named after the fourth-century Church Father, John Chrysostom, who wrote some of the finest sermons ever recorded. Those eighteen authors have pledged to carry on the highest quality of writing possible. The group includes people like Philip Yancey, Eugene Peterson, Calvin Miller, and Emilie Griffin. Richard Foster is included among them as well. These eighteen writers joined together and wrote a wonderful book in 1990 called, *Reality and the Vision*. Each of these contemporary Christian writers takes their turn in describing who has helped them form their faith. I deeply appreciate all of the chapters, but it is Foster's piece that spoke most deeply to me. He entitled his chapter, "The Devotional Masters: A Love Affair."

Richard says it was desperation that led him to the Devotional Masters. He was serving a small congregation in Southern California and noticed that "nothing seemed to lead us into experiencing the depths of Jesus Christ" (*Reality and the Vision*, p. 80). It was out of that despair when he "turned" to his neglected friends like Bonhoeffer, Augustine, Juliana of Norwich, Francis of Assisi, John Woolman, and Jean-Pierre de Caussade. I admit that not all those he mentions are monks in the classical sense of that word, but all are monklike in the sense of a wholehearted pursuit of experiencing the depths of Jesus. They became his teachers and he became the hungry student. The encouragement that

Foster's example has brought to me is unspeakable. His candid and refreshing honesty about his own struggle has cheered me on to continue learning from the great ones of the past. I love how Richard concludes his chapter. "Over the years desperation has turned to delight and delight has turned to a deep and abiding friendship—a love affair with the Masters. I invite you to join me" (*Reality*, p. 91).

May I put my small voice alongside all those other voices? Join us on this journey worth taking. Evelyn Underhill read and studied Augustine, Catherine of Siena, Julian of Norwich, Lawrence, Woolman, Fox, Wesley, and many others. She said that their books had the ability to remove all of us from the spiritual potato fields where we live and labor, and remind us of the mountains and the sea! "These books are never finished and done with. . . . Such reading, if properly done, is really a form of prayer" (*Concerning the Inner Life*, p.33). Find a great saint from the past. Dig deeply into his life and words. See how he points us ever closer to Jesus. Listen to what the monks can teach us.

> May I put my small voice alongside all those other voices? Join us on this journey worth taking. Listen to what the monks can teach us.

Works Cited

Athanasius. *The Life of St. Antony.* New York: Newman Press, 1978.

Augustine. *The Confessions of St. Augustine.* New York: Image Books, 1960.

Barth, Karl. *Dogmatics in Outline.* New York: Harper and Row, 1959.

Bellah, Robert. *Habits of the Heart.* Berkeley: University of California Press, 1985.

Benedict. *The Rule of St. Benedict in English.* Collegeville, MN: The Liturgical Press, 1982.

Bloesch, Donald. "A Call to Spirituality." *The Orthodox Evangelicals.* Ed. by Robert Webber and Donald Bloesch. Nashville: Nelson, 1978.

_____. *The Crisis of Piety.* Colorado Springs, CO: Helmers and Howard, 1988.

Bloom, Allan. *The Closing of the American Mind.* New York: Simon and Schuster, 1987.

Bonhoeffer, Dietrich. *The Cost of Discipleship.* New York: Macmillan and Collier, 1963.

_____. *A Testament of Freedom.* Ed. by Geffrey Kelley and Burton Nelson. San Francisco: Harper, 1990.

Brother Lawrence. *The Practice of the Presence of God.* Mt. Vernon, NY: Peter Pauper, 1963.

Bultmann, Rudolf. *Kerygma and Myth.* Vol. 1. Trans. by R.H. Fuller. London: SPCK, 1953.

Cahill, Thomas. *How the Irish Saved Civilization.* New York: Doubleday, 1995.

Carney, Glandion. *Heaven within These Walls*. Ventura, CA: Regal Books, 1989.

Clapp, Rodney. "Remonking the Church." *Christianity Today*, August 12, 1988.

Colson, Chuck. *Against the Night*. Ann Arbor: Servant Publications, 1989.

Elliot, Elizabeth. *Passion and Purity*. Old Tappen, NJ: Fleming H. Revell, 1984.

Farmer, David. *Oxford Dictionary of Saints*. New York: Oxford University Press, 1997.

Foster, Richard. *Celebration of Discipline*. New York: Harper, 1978.

Goldberg, Louis. "Bin." *Theological Wordbook of the Old Testament*. Vol. 1. Ed. by R. Laird Hanes, Gleason J. Archer, and Bruce K. Waltke. Chicago: Moody Bible Institute, 1980.

Guinness, Os. *The Gravedigger File*. Downers Grove, IL: InterVarsity, 1983.

Kettler, Christian. *The Vicarious Humanity of Christ and the Reality of Salvation*. Lanham, MD: University Press of America, 1991.

Kierkegaard, Søren. *Christian Discourses*. Princeton, NJ: Princeton University Press, 1971.

Knowles, David. *Christian Monasticism*. New York: McGraw-Hill, 1968.

Latourette, Kenneth. *Christianity through the Ages*. New York: Harper and Chapel Books, 1965.

Lewis, C.S. *The Screwtape Letters*. New York: Macmillan, 1961.

Luther, Martin. *Three Treatises.* Philadelphia: Fortress Press, 1970.

Maxwell, John, and Jim Dornan. *Becoming a Person of Influence.* Nashville: Nelson, 1997.

McNamara, Jo Ann. "Inside the Convent." *Church History.* Vol. 10. No. 2. Carol Stream, IL: Christianity Today, 1991.

Merton, Thomas. *The Sign of Jonas.* Garden City, NJ: Doubleday and Image Books, 1956.

Miller, Calvin. *Into the Depths of God.* Minneapolis: Bethany House, 2000.

Muto, Susan Annette. *A Practical Guide to Spiritual Reading.* Danville, NJ: Dimension Books, 1976.

Nouwen, Henri. "Silence: The Portable Cell." *Sojourners.* July, 1980.

Pennington, Basil. *Light from the Cloister.* Mahwah, NJ: Paulist Press, 1991.

Peterson, Eugene. *The Contemplative Pastor.* Carol Stream, IL: Christianity Today, 1989.

_____. *Earth and Altar.* Downers Grove, IL: InterVarsity, 1985.

_____. *Five Smooth Stones for Pastoral Work.* Atlanta: John Knox Press, 1980.

_____. *Take and Read.* Grand Rapids: Eerdmans, 1996.

_____. *Working the Angles.* Grand Rapids: Eerdmans, 1987.

Postman, Neil. *Amusing Ourselves to Death.* New York: Penguin Books, 1986.

W
O
R
K
S

C
I
T
E
D

Stott, John R.W. *The Cross of Christ.* Downers Grove, IL: InterVarsity, 1986.

Tickle, Phyllis. *The Divine Hours.* New York: Doubleday, 2001.

Torrence, Thomas F. *The Trinitarian Faith.* Edinburgh: T & T Clark, 1988.

Tozer, A.W. *The Pursuit of God.* Camp Hill, PA: Christian Publications, 1982.

_____. *The Size of the Soul.* Camp Hill, PA: Christian Publications, 1996.

_____. *That Incredible Christian.* Camp Hill, PA: Christian Publications, 1986.

Tucker, Ruth. "Heloise and Abelard's Tumultuous Affair." *Christian History.* Vol. 1. No. 2. Carol Stream, IL: Christianity Today, 1991.

Underhill, Evelyn. *Concerning the Inner Life and The House of the Soul.* Minneapolis: Winston-Seabury Press, 1929.

Veith, Gene. *Postmodern Times: A Christian Guide to Contemporary Thought and Culture.* Wheaton: Crossway, 1994.

Walker, Helen. *Knights of Christ.* Englewood Cliffs, NJ: Prentice-Hall, 1957.

Ware, Corinne. *St. Benedict on the Freeway.* Nashville: Abingdon Press, 2001.

Warren, Ann. "Five Religious Options for Medieval Women." *Christian History.* Vol. 10. No. 2. May, 1991.

Weidmann, Jim, and Joe White. *Spiritual Mentoring of Teens.* Wheaton: Tyndale House, 2001.

**W
O
R
K
S

C
I
T
E
D**